ENEMIES OF THE
BLESSINGS OF
RIGHTEOUSNESS

*Lisa, be blessed
and enjoy reading.
I thank God for you.*

*Love,
Amelia P. Young
2017*

ENEMIES OF THE BLESSINGS OF RIGHTEOUSNESS

The Importance of Guarding Your Heart

ENEMIES OF THE BLESSINGS OF RIGHTEOUSNESS

Published by Forever Young Publishing Co.
© 2017 by Amelia P. Young. All rights reserved.

Enemies of the Blessings of Righteousness

ISBN 978-1544056906

This book is available at quantity discounts for bulk purchases.

Printed in the United States of America.

All scripture references and quotations, unless otherwise indicated, are taken from the Holy Bible – King James and New International Versions

Book Cover Art by Amelia P. Young

Cover design and book production:
Amelia P. Young, LaVerne Harris &
Loretta Norris

IV

To wit, that God was in Christ, reconciling the world unto himself, not imputing their trespasses unto them; and hath committed unto us the word of reconciliation.

Now then we are ambassadors for Christ, as though God did beseech you by us: we pray you in Christ's stead, be ye reconciled to God.

For he hath made him to be sin for us, who knew no sin; that we might be made the righteousness of God in him.

II Corinthians 5:19-21

DEDICATION

It is with love and gratitude that I dedicate this book to everyone who will embrace the truths it holds.

ACKNOWLEDGEMENTS

I give all honor and praise to my Heavenly Father for yet another expression of His love, power and provision in my life. I could not have accomplished this or any other offering of hope without His grace and favor.

I also acknowledge and I'm grateful for and to every person (friend or foe), for every experience, and every trial that has molded me into the person I am becoming in the Lord. To each of you, I say thank you.

I acknowledge the guidance of the Holy Spirit of God in this experience. It has truly heightened my trust and love for God. As I live in His presence daily, my prayer is that I will continue to enjoy the blessings living righteously offers to me and each of us.

I also thank God for the loving and lasting freindship and sisterhood I share with LaVerne Harris. Her insight and input in this endeavor is invaluable.

FOOTSTEPS OF THE RIGHTEOUS

The steps of a good man are ordered by the Lord, (Psa. 37:23). This man is blessed of the Lord; his steps which he takes in life are ordered/ordained by the Lord, both with the physical and the spiritual things he encounters. But know for a surety that this good man's behavior is not of himself, it is yet another blessing from the Lord, who directs and keeps the feet of his saints.

We can be sure that the Lord directs the steps of the godly. He delights in every detail of their lives. Though they stumble, they will never utterly fall, for the Lord himself holds them by his protective hand (Isa. 40:29-31). It is both amazing and comforting to know that God walks with us, leading and ordering each step we take, and to know that the Lord delights in us.

God is in, has been in, and forever will be in the business of watching over and bringing guidance to the lives of His faithful followers who believe in Him... who will obeyHim, love and follow Him with their whole hearts and lives (Psa. 119:2).

God's hand over us is often incomprehensible, even overlooked at times... like a loving parent who stands in the background watching over His child, not interfering with their freedom to make their own decisions. Yet, He is there with us quietly directing the details of every step we make as He promised to do. Not only is His watchful eye upon us, His ear stands ready to hear our every cry. His protective hand is also there to help if we should stumble and fall.

REMEMBER: "We can make our plans, but only the Lord determines our steps."

CONTENTS

FOREWORD
By Rev. Eric Wilson, Sr.

The adversity and opposition encountered by the Christians of this age are of the same level and intensity as suffered by Christ Jesus himself. Satan's tactics and strategies have evolved to hinder today's believers but his wrath is equally as venomous as it was in the Garden of Eden centuries ago. Alternative religions like Buddhism, Muslim, Hinduism, Atheism, compete for the lives and souls of men and women today. Pseudo-Christian beliefs such as Mormonism, Jehovah Witnesses, and Scientology offer unstable belief systems that challenge promises to Christians of eternal life by offering immediate rewards for discipleship. Extreme terrorist groups like ISIL, Boko Haram, Hezbollah, Al Qaeda, and the Mujahedeen literally target, violently, I might add, societies and countries anchored in Christianity. Toxic institutions like entertainment, politics, Wall Street, education, the criminal justice system, and a tension filled foreign policy offer only panic and unrest to all of mankind on a daily basis. Even though we (as Christians) know victory is ours, and are prepared to declare victory will be ours, it is still extremely essential for us to be reminded that our righteousness (our right standing with God) comes with a very deep, deep well of blessings.

Righteousness, our right standing with God, is enjoyed, without compromise, by believers because of the redemptive work of our Lord and Savior Jesus Christ. This righteousness is not a description of our behavior, for we do sin occasionally. This righteousness describes our position with God to be one of right standing, therefore reconciled and redeemed for all eternity.

"Enemies of the Blessings of Righteousness" seeks to remind and cause us all to reflect that there are enemies to all of the blessings that come with that righteousness. Amelia Young adequately runs this leg of the Christian race by accurately identifying challenges, hindrances and oppositions, both external and internal to those blessings. She has clearly captured, in print, the perspective of every born again believer and by writing this book creates a tangible tool of introspective review, a baton so to speak, that can be passed on to generations to come!

To God Be The Glory For The Good Things He Has Done!

INTRODUCTION

The goal and desire of every born-again Christian should be to live a life that glorifies God; a life that allows the Spirit of God to move freely within it. It is impossible to achieve such a goal without the help of the Holy Spirit's involvement in our everyday behavior. A person cannot experience the level of fellowship which God desires until he accepts God's salvation and be conformed to the image of Christ Jesus. Therefore, Christian maturity fulfills the desires of both God and man.

It is with that fact in mind that I have written this book. May the Holy Spirit of God enlighten the hearts and minds of each reader as he/she, believer and non-believer, lets the light of God's Word in and allows that light to dictate their actions. May they seek to live in God's presence daily, trusting His Word and His way for their life and obeying Him. These are all necessary to make this journey of righteousness possible and to receive all the blessings associated with it. May you choose to walk and live a life resembling the righteousness God has showered upon us as we explore the subjects listed herein.

FOR YOUR READING:

II Corinthians 5:21 *God made him who had no sin to be sin for us, so that in him we might become the righteousness of God.*

I Timothy 6:11 *But thou, O man of God, flee these things; and follow after righteousness, godliness, faith, love, patience, meekness.*

Psalm 11:7 *For the righteous LORD loveth righteousness; his countenance doth behold the upright.*

FEAR

Fear: noun - a distressing emotion aroused by impending danger, evil, pain, etc., whether the threat is real or imagined; the feeling or condition of being afraid.

The Bible tells us in II Timothy 1:7 that "God has not given us the spirit of fear (timidity, cowardice); but of power (boldness), and of love, and of a sound mind (sensibleness, wisdom, sound judgment and self-discipline)." When we operate in any way other than in power, love and a sound mind, we are walking outside of the will of God. Because of reverence to God, walking in power and love and a sound mind makes sense.

God's Holy Spirit was given to us to guide us and lead us in all righteousness and truth. If we allow fear to rule our relationships with others and with God, we are saying that God's way is not the best way. Thus – we are to let go of the fear that causes us to overlook the sins that keep us from receiving the full extent of the power God wants us to operate in. We must love what God loves and hate what He hates. Romans 6:2 says: "God forbid. How shall we, that are dead to sin, live any longer there in?"

When we are anxious about things, we are taking God's place in our lives. He has promised to keep us in perfect peace, (Phil 4:6) when we believe his promise, we experience His peace. This peace does not come as the world dictates, by having money and the things it can

1

buy. Trusting God brings peace to the believer. Fear snuffs out the peace that wants to reside and saturate our lives.

PRAYER: Lord, give us the wisdom to truly trust you in all things and at all times. Help us not be afraid to totally allow the Holy Spirit to guide our lives. Grant us boldness to embrace your plan for our lives as it unfolds moment by moment. Amen.

INSIGHT: The danger of being fearful is that we miss out on all the good things God has planned for our lives. When we don't trust God, His Spirit and His Word, we are blinded by our own choosing. In other words: we leave countless blessings on the table. Romans 8:28 "And we know that all things work together for good to them that love God, to them who are the called according to his purpose." I want everything God wants to bless me with. How about you?

FEAR IS A ROBBER

Life has been given to you
And given abundantly
To live with gratitude in your heart to love humanity

Fear robs you of the joy and happiness
That new life in Christ brings
Silencing expressions of love and praises
your heart wants to sing

Anxiety comes with baggage
That unfolds past mistakes
Making you think you are worthless
Keeping doubts alive and fears wide-awake

Sensibility, wisdom, soundness of mind
and self-discipline are the gifts God will give
When you decide it is for God you will live

Fear has no place in the life
of a child of the King
Who covers them with His Righteousness
Withholding from them no good thing

FEAR

Forfeiting

Every

Advantage

Righteousness affords

FOR YOUR READING:
Psalm 27:3 *Though an host should encamp against me, my heart shall not fear: though war should rise against me, in this will I be confident.;*

Psalm 46:2 *Therefore will not we fear, though the earth be removed, and though the mountains be carried into the midst of the sea;*

Psalm 56:4 *In God I will praise his word, in God I have put my trust; I will not fear what flesh can do unto me.*
Psalm 118:6 *The LORD is on my side; I will not fear: what can man do unto me?*

Proverbs 19:23 *The foolishness of man perverteth his way: and his heart fretteth against the LORD.*

Hebrews 13:6 *So that we may boldly say, The Lord is my helper, and I will not fear what man shall do unto me.*

I John 4:18 *There is no fear in love; but perfect love casteth out fear: because fear hath torment. He that feareth is not made perfect in love.*

Psalms 27:1-6 *The LORD is my light and my salvation; whom shall I fear? the LORD is the strength of my life; of whom shall I be afraid? When the wicked, even mine enemies and my foes, came upon me to eat up my flesh, they stumbled and fell. Though an host should encamp against me, my heart shall not fear: though war should rise against me, in this will I be confident.*

One thing have I desired of the LORD, that will I seek after; that I may dwell in the house of the LORD all the days of my life, to behold the beauty of the LORD, and to inquire in his temple. For in the time of trouble he shall hide me in his pavilion: in the secret of his tabernacle shall he hide me; he shall set me up upon a rock. And now shall mine head be lifted up above mine enemies round about me: therefore will I offer in his tabernacle sacrifices of joy; I will sing, yea, I will sing praises unto the LORD.

THOUGHT: The Believer's peace of mind is not just the absence of fear and troubles, but the presence of hope and confidence that the Word of God gives.

My advice to you --- Fear Not!

RESENTMENT

Resentment: noun - the feeling of displeasure or indignation at some act, remark, person, etc., regarded as causing injury or insult.

We cannot be righteous (right with God) and harbor resentment toward others. Resentment blocks our growth in the ways of God and it causes ill feelings and strife in our relationships, not to mention the damage it does to our own health and well being. I am not saying that we are not allowed to oppose things that are unacceptable, but we have to look at them like Jesus would – with love. Ephesians 4:26 says: "Be ye angry, and sin not: let not the sun go down upon your wrath:"

Resentments that are allowed to linger in our hearts are likely to escalate into something more damaging to our righteousness. We cannot afford to allow the enemy to cause us to entertain resentments that soon intensify into bitterness and ultimately hatred – a zone the child of God must not enter.

Other words related to resentment are: grievance, score, and grudge. With grievances comes complaints, and distress. Scores are marks used for keeping count of unfavorable things. Just say and listen to the word "grudge", it sounds like it will do damage all by the way it sounds. To have a grudge means you are unwilling to give in or forgive.

7

PRAYER: Lord, help us keep our hearts and minds free from resentments. Help us look at things and others as you would. Don't let us harbor ill feelings toward our fellow man. Let us be quick to forgive and thus, be imitators of you. Amen

INSIGHT: When we hold on to hurts and offences we encounter; we are at risk of them poisoning our spirit. It becomes inevitable that we will suffer even more injury than the original offense. Harboring resentment toward another is like taking poison and expecting it not to affect us. Proverbs 14:21-22 "He that despiseth his neighbour sinneth: but he that hath mercy on the poor, happy is he. Do they not err that devise evil? but mercy and truth shall be to them that devise good."

THOUGHT: "Holding resentment is like eating poison and waiting for the other person to keel over."~ Unknown

RESENTMENT

(Indignation or ill will felt as a result of a real or imagined grievance)

Resentment is a waste of precious time
That focuses on the offense
It takes our eyes off forgiveness
And makes us subject to sin's consequence

Devising ways to get even
That might satisfy our selfish whim
Forgetting who lives inside us
And causing our light to dim

Own your feelings
Even if they are feelings of hurt
But letting them remain unacknowledged
Will give them cause to pervert

Guard your heart
And the life God wants for you
Be quick to let go of things
That will alter your rational view

Only God can even the score
And make all things right
Yes, you are in a battle
But remember, the battle is not yours to fight

Don't waste time resenting!
Spend time trusting and praying to God
Taking Him all your hurts and cares
Making getting over resentments not so hard

REMEMBER: When you experience painful emotions, acknowledge them, even make them known to the offender if you have to. Trying to ignore them or bury them won't make them dissolve or go away. They could build up over time and turn into resentment.

INSIGHT: Resentments are directly attracted to hurts. The impact of holding on to them can be deadly to both parties involved— the one who is hurting and the one causing the hurt.

FOR YOUR READING:
Proverbs 10:12 *Hatred stirreth up strifes: but love covereth all sins.*

Leviticus 19:18 *Thou shalt not avenge, nor bear any grudge against the children of thy people, but thou shalt love thy neighbour as thyself: I am the LORD.*

James 5:9 *Grudge not one against another, brethren, lest ye be condemned: behold, the judge standeth before the door.*

UNFORGIVING

Unforgiving: adj - unwillingness to forgive.

A believer who walks in unforgiveness undermines righteousness in every way possible. It is as if he chooses to dress in the enemy's too-tight clothing and ill-fitting shoes and expect God not to notice him.

Forgiveness is such an incredibly powerful gift from God given to be used by the believer in their daily lives. God knew that there would always be something to forgive, so He equipped us with the tool we would need to get the job done— Faith. Faith in God to be able to forgive, even when we think it is impossible. We are most like God when we choose to forgive rather than hold a grudge. However, the first barrier to be removed where forgiveness is concerned is within ourselves, and it starts with making a choice to forgive. Focus on the hurt or offense doesn't allow reconciliation to happen, it will only feed anger.

How can we expect God to forgive us our trespasses when we are unwilling to do the same for others? The bible tells us in Matthew 6:14-15: "For if ye forgive men their trespasses, your heavenly Father will also forgive you: But if ye forgive not men their trespasses, neither will your Father forgive your trespasses."

Unforgiveness in a person is like a cancer that grows worse and worse. Eventually killing all rational thinking, compassion, gladness, tranquility, tolerance, kindness, belief and many other things that are needed

11

to walk in rightness with God. Look at what the Bible tells us that should be operating in us. "But the fruit of the Spirit is love, joy, peace, longsuffering, gentleness, goodness, faith, meekness, temperance: against such there is no law." Galatians 5:22-23

Forgiveness is thought to be for the offender but I think it is more for the offended. When you choose to forgive someone for an offense done to you, your healing process begins. Unforgiveness on the other hand is like taking poison and expecting the offender to die from it. When you harbor ill fillings for another person it hurts you, adding to your already painful situation.

Don't be guilty of being unforgiving. Remember your forgiveness hinges upon your ability to forgive others. Even if the other person never repents or asks for forgiveness, it is wise for us to forgive them anyway. Ask yourself this question, "Will forgiving this person please God?" The answer will always be "Yes."

PRAYER:

Forgive us O Lord our
trespasses as we forgive others of their's.
Show us what it is that adds
purpose to this life we live,
and what shapes our thoughts and actions
and helps us to forgive.
For we want to do all that you
expect of us each and every day.
We never want to be a disobedient child
or ever go astray. Amen

INSIGHT: Our relationships are with people and people come with the potential to hurt us. We too, have the potential to hurt others. But we have an equalizer, if we so choose to use it. It is Forgiveness. God's Spirit has equipped us with the power of reconciliation as seen in II Corinthians 5: 18-19. "And all things are of God, who hath reconciled us to himself by Jesus Christ, and hath given to us the ministry of reconciliation; To wit, that God was in Christ, reconciling the world unto himself, not imputing their trespasses unto them; and hath committed unto us the word of reconciliation."

FOR YOUR READING:
Leviticus 19:18 *Thou shalt not avenge, nor bear any grudge against the children of thy people, but thou shalt love thy neighbour as thyself: I am the LORD.*

Matthew 6:14-15 *For if ye forgive men their trespasses, your heavenly Father will also forgive you: But if ye forgive not men their trespasses, neither will your Father forgive your trespasses.*

Colossians 3:12-13 *Put on therefore, as the elect of God, holy and beloved, bowels of mercies, kindness, humbleness of mind, meekness, longsuffering; Forbearing one another, and forgiving one another, if any man have a quarrel against any: even as Christ forgave you, so also do ye.*

Mark 11:25 *And when ye stand praying, forgive, if ye have aught against any; that your Father also which is in heaven may forgive you your trespasses.*

THOUGHTS:

"To err is human, to forgive, divine." ~ Alexander Pope

"To forgive is to set a prisoner free and discover that the prisoner was you." ~ Lewis B. Smedes

"To forgive is the highest, most beautiful form of love. In return, you will receive untold peace and happiness." ~ Robert Muller

"The weak can never forgive. Forgiveness is the attribute of the strong." ~ Mahatma Gandhi

"Forgiveness does not change the past, but it does enlarge the future." ~ Paul Boose

IF YOU PLANT

If you plant unforgiveness,
unforgiveness will grow
Your harvest will only be a result
of the seeds you sow
Forgiveness does not excuse
the hurt you have been dealt
But when you release pardon,
the pain just starts to melt
It's your choice to release it or refuse
To begin the healing process,
the hurt and pain to lose
You are the one who needs to call
forgiveness into view
For it is not just for the offender,
it is mainly for you
Somehow you get stuck in
the hurt that you feel
Making everything around you
seem so unreal
When you stop feeling the joy
that Jesus gives
Soon you find you cease to really live

If you plant unforgiveness,
unforgiveness will grow
Your harvest will only be a result
of the seeds you sow
What seeds are you planting in
your life's garden today?

Herein Jesus teaches the art of forgiveness. "Lord, how many times shall I forgive my brother or sister who sins against me? Up to seven times?" Jesus answered, "I tell you, not seven times, but seventy times seven" (Matthew 18:21-22.) Does this mean we are to forgive 490 times in a day? Yes, and more of necessary.

The Believer has been given the blessing of a measure of faith fashioned just for them. Matthew 12:3 "For I say, through the grace given unto me, to every man that is among you, not to think of himself more highly than he ought to think; but to think soberly, according as God hath dealt to every man the measure of faith." It is up to each one to grow that faith according to Hebrews 10:17, "So then faith cometh by hearing, and hearing by the word of God." If mustard seed size faith is powerful enough to move mountains (Matthew 17:20), how much more could we do with a growing faith? Faith to remove all the obstacles placed in your path by offenses of others. Only forgiveness can do this.

REMEMBER: If we are unwilling to forgive, our Heavenly Father will not forgive us.

- Forgiveness is not easy, but it is possible.
- Forgiveness requires the power of the Holy Spirit.
- Forgiveness is primarily for YOU, not just for the other person involved.
- Forgiveness frees you to get on with living right with God and man.
- Forgiveness opens your heart to reconcilation.
- Forgiveness is what God desires.

UNTRUTH

Untruth: noun - the state or character of being untrue. 2. want of veracity; divergence from truth. 3. something untrue; a falsehood or lie. Synonyms: fiction, story, tale, fabrication, invention.

Since God's Word is truth, anything that opposes God's Word would be untruth. There is no way we can manipulate the truth to suit our circumstances without trespassing against God. When we say, act, or conclude anything that is false we are not following the principals laid down in God's Word. Colossians 3:9-10 says, "Lie not one to another, seeing that ye have put off the old man with his deeds; And have put on the new man, which is renewed in knowledge after the image of him that created him."

Righteous living demands that we live the truth not just some of the time, but all the time. Why? Because God is Truth and the Bible declares that if we are of God, we would know the truth and that truth would make us free; free to live holy lives, free to make right decisions, and free to be honest and open in our dealings with others. John 8:32, "And ye shall know the truth, and the truth shall make you free.

We lighten the gravity of lies when we or others refer to them as "little white lies, fibs, fabrications, stories and such." They are still untruths/lies, devices of darkness. Call it what it is – a lie/untruth.

18

Truth however, causes us to walk in the light. Untruths destroy fellowship, friendship and all other relationships. Making it impossible to live righteously among our fellowman and God. The side-effects from lies can linger in our lives for years, causing all types of difficulties, complications, and makes us appear untrustworthy.

These prayers to God by King David for both protection from his enemies and protection from sin is a good prayer for saints today...

> Show me your ways, O LORD,
> teach me your paths;
> guide me in your truth and teach me,
> for you are God my Savior,
> and my hope is in you all day long. . . .
> Guard my life and rescue me;
> let me not be put to shame,
> for I take refuge in you.
> May integrity and uprightness protect me,
> because my hope is in you. (Psalm 25:4-5, 20-21)

> Set a guard over my mouth, O LORD;
> keep watch over the door of my lips.
> Let not my heart be drawn to what is evil,
> to take part in wicked deeds
> let me not eat of their delicacies. (Psalm 141:3-4)

PRAYER: Father, help us to desire with all our hearts the ability to walk humbly and truthfully with you in our daily lives. Give us the hearts to follow wholly after you and seek your ways. Teach us to be people of truth. Cause us to seek after holiness because we know that you are Truth and you are Holy. Don't just keep us safe," but "Lord, keep us pure." In Jesus name, amen.

FOR YOUR READING:
John 1:14 *And the Word was made flesh, and dwelt among us, (and we beheld his glory, the glory as of the only begotten of the Father,) full of grace and truth.*

I John 1:6 *If we say that we have fellowship with him and walk in the darkness, we lie, and do not the truth:*

Psalms 15:1-2 *Lord, who shall abide in thy tabernacle? who shall dwell in thy holy hill? He that walketh uprightly, and worketh righteousness, and speaketh the truth in his heart.*

Colossians 3:9-10 *Lie not one to another, seeing that ye have put off the old man with his deeds; And have put on the new man, which is renewed in knowledge after the image of him that created him:*

Proverbs 12:22 *Lying lips are an abomination to the LORD: but they that deal truly are his delight.*

James 1:21-27 *Therefore put away all filthiness and rampant wickedness and receive with meekness the implanted word, which is able to save your souls. But be doers of the word, and not hearers only, deceiving yourselves. For if anyone is a hearer of the word and not a doer, he is like a man who looks intently at his natural face in a mirror. For he looks at himself and goes away and at once forgets what he was like. But the one who looks into the perfect law, the law of liberty, and perseveres, being no hearer who forgets but a doer who acts, he will be blessed in his doing. If anyone thinks he is religious and does not bridle his tongue but deceives his heart, this person's religion is worthless. ...*

DECEPTION

Deception: noun - the act of deceiving; the state of being deceived. 2. something that deceives or is intended to deceive; fraud; cunning devices.

Deception is akin to untruth and lies. Just listen to words that describe it - beguilement, deceit, trickery, concealment, mystification, ruse and subterfuge, ploy. These are all used to deceive and make a lie look true. This is easily accomplished when the whole truth is not conveyed. The height of deception is when one sets out to make another believe through trickery or by saying one thing and meaning something totally different.

Deception is a major offense in any relationship. Whether in friendships, marriages or working relationships, deception will bring about destruction. It most surely will lead to feelings of betrayal and distrust between partners and ultimately cause separation. Deception always violates the rules and is considered to be a truce-breaker. No relationship can thrive when deception is practiced.

No one likes to be tricked, especially when he or she realizes they have been tricked into believing something that is not the truth. Somehow that fact alone makes the entire ordeal a cause for great embarrassment and hurt.

There are always those who would take advantage of others by teaching and advocating lies for truth. It is our place as followers of Christ to seek His ways and walk in them daily. This will make us less likely to fall victim to false teachings.

FOR YOUR READING:

Matthew 24:4-5 *And Jesus answered and said unto them, take heed that no man deceive you. For many shall come in my name, saying, I am Christ; and shall deceive many.*

Matthew 24:11 *And many false prophets shall rise, and shall deceive many.*

Matthew 24:24-25 *For there shall arise false Christs, and false prophets, and shall shew great signs and wonders; insomuch that, if it were possible, they shall deceive the very elect. Behold, I have told you before.*

Ephesians 5:6; 2 Thessalonians 2:3 *Little children, let no man deceive you: he that doeth righteousness is righteous, even as he is righteous.*

Proverbs 24:28 *Be not a witness against thy neighbour without cause; and deceive not with thy lips.*

Galatians 6:3 *For if a man think himself to be something, when he is nothing, he deceiveth himself.*

I Tim 3:13 But evil men and seducers shall wax worse and worse, deceiving, and being deceived.

Colossians 3:9-10 *Lie not one to another, seeing that you have put off the old man with his deeds. And have put on the new man, which is renewed in knowledge after the image of him that created him.*

PRAYER: Let Psalms 139:23-24 be your heart's cry today;

Search me, O God, and know my heart today; Try me, O Savior, know my thoughts I pray. See if there be some wicked way in me; Cleanse me from every sin and set me free.

ENVY

Envy: noun - A feeling of discontent and resentment aroused by and in conjunction with desire for the possessions, advantages, successes or qualities of another.

Envy is akin to jealousy. With envy, you feel resentful because someone has something you desire. With jealousy, you feel someone is trying to take something away that you have. They are two of the most common but are, by far, the most useless and negative of emotions. To envy or be jealous of someone, you most likely, have determined that what you have is not good enough or just plain enough. You want more, more than you rightfully deserve. If allowed, these two emotions will prove to be both destructive and poisonous to your own well-being.

When we envy people, we waste precious time that can be spent on things that can grow us in Christ. Envy makes us start to unravel the good things God wants to do in our lives because of our want of what someone else has. We then become prisoners of our greed and cease to be the person God wants us to be. We let what others do and what they have determine how we feel about our lives; mostly inadequate, not what God has purposed for us. Doesn't His Word teach us to find contentment in what we have? (Philippians 4:11)

If left unchecked or unmanaged, envy can stunt our growth to spiritual maturity and lead us to destructive behavior.

We are not to envy what the next person has because it displeases our Heavenly Father when we look upon another's possessions with a heart to gain it for ourselves. Thus, forgetting or overlooking blessings our God has blessed us with.

Most of the time when we feel envious, we really don't want what the other person has, we simply do not want them to have it. Being envious blinds us from seeing how truly blessed we are already.

Remember, being a child of God, you have access to the riches of God through doing the right thing and living in harmony with God. He will generously bestow His blessings abundantly upon you as you walk in obedience to His will. These blessings of God take away the need to envy anything anyone else has. Our God knows what we need and even gives us some of the desires of our hearts.

FOR YOUR READING:

Proverbs 23:17 *Let not thy heart envy sinners, but [be thou] in the fear of Jehovah all the day;*

Deuteronomy 5:21 *Neither shalt thou desire thy neighbour's wife, neither shalt thou covet thy neighbour's house, his field, nor his bondman, nor his handmaid, his ox, nor his ass, nor anything that is thy neighbour's.*

Matthew 6: 31-32 *Therefore take no thought, saying, What shall we eat? or, What shall we drink? or,*

Wherewithal shall we be clothed? (For after all these things do the Gentiles seek:) for your heavenly Father knoweth that ye have need of all these things.

Psalms 37:4-6 *Delight thyself also in the LORD: and he shall give thee the desires of thine heart. Commit thy way unto the LORD; trust also in him; and he shall bring it to pass. And he shall bring forth thy righteousness as the light, and thy judgment as the noonday.*

Hebrews 13:5 *Let your conversation be without covetousness; and be content with such things as ye have: for he hath said, I will never leave thee, nor forsake thee.*

Exodus 20:17 *Thou shalt not covet thy neighbour's house, thou shalt not covet thy neighbour's wife, nor his manservant, nor his maidservant, nor his ox, nor his ass, nor any thing that is thy neighbour's.*

NO NEED TO ENVY

Envy blinds you to the beauty and uniqueness God
placed in you alone.
Giving birth to greed for things of others
from the seed your jealousy has sewn

Wanting things the physical eye beholds
and ignoring what is within
Causing thoughts of inadequacy and lack
making room for you to sin

Delight yourself in God instead
for in Him are the desires of your heart
You will love the masterpiece He has made
One of a kind, setting you apart

Never again will you have to
envy, fear or despair
Because you will know for certainty
You are always in His care

HATRED

Hatred: noun - the feeling of one who hates; intense dislike or extreme aversion or hostility.

I don't quite know when I learned this little poem, but I sure am glad I did. It is simple but so full of truth.

Hate destroys the vessel
in which it is stored
Much more than on the vessel
on which it is poured
(Author unknown)

In other words, when we allow hatred to rule in our hearts, we are more infected and affected by it than the objects of our hatred. It's like ingesting strychnine and hoping it kills the person we hate.

Hatred works against the love and compassion that should be ruling the heart. Even more damaging, it blocks the righteousness God placed in the believer from doing its perfect work. This is like bad ingredients in certain processed foods that work against the good nutrition it promises. We take the time to check labels for the best foods for ourselves and our family's health, but we don't think twice when it comes to unleashing hateful behavior on others.

Hatred is not of God. It stands in total opposition to Love which characterizes who God is. I John 4:7-8 "Beloved, let us love one another; because love is of God, and every one that loves has been begotten of God, and knows God. He that loves not has not known God; for God is love."

PRAYER: And this I pray, that your love may abound yet more and more in knowledge and in all judgment; That ye may approve things that are excellent; that ye may be sincere and without offense till the day of Christ; Being filled with the fruits of righteousness, which are by Jesus Christ, unto the glory and praise of God. Philippians 1:9-11

FOR YOUR READING:
I John 4:20-21 *If anyone say, I love God, and hate his brother, he is a liar: for he that loves not his brother whom he has seen, how can he love God whom he has not seen? And this commandment have we from him, that he that loves God love also his brother.*

Proverbs 10:12 *Hatred stirreth up strifes; but love covereth all transgressions.*

JEALOUSY

Jealousy: noun - jealous resentment against a rival, a person enjoying success or advantage, etc., or against another's success or advantage itself. 2. mental uneasiness from suspicion or fear of rivalry, unfaithfulness, etc.

This enemy of the blessings of righteousness starts with a dissatisfaction within one's heart. When someone else achieves things in their lives and another doesn't seem to be able to achieve anything, the door is then opened to feelings of jealousy. Saying it is hard to find people that are happy at your success is an understatement. Being satisfied with how wonderfully God has made you is the first step to not falling prey to the evils of jealousy.

Setting goals and doing something every day concerning those goals will help to achieve them. But wasting time being jealous of someone who has achieved their goals will only cause heartache and frustration. All those negative thoughts will cause unrighteousness to rear its ugly head and damage your relationship with a Holy God who expects holiness from us. He has equipped us for greatness. Being jealous of someone else is both foolish and a waste of precious time—time you could be using to accomplish goals in your own life.

Since jealousy is such a powerful enemy of righteousness, we need God's Word to help us ward off its effects. Hopefully the following few scriptures will help.

FOR YOUR READING:

James 3:14-16 *But if ye have bitter envying and strife in your hearts, glory not, and lie not against the truth. This wisdom descendeth not from above, but is earthly, sensual, devilish. For where envying and strife is, there is confusion and every evil work.*

Proverbs 6:34-35 *For jealousy is the rage of a man: therefore, he will not spare in the day of vengeance. He will not regard any ransom; neither will he rest content, though thou givest many gifts.*

Colossians 1:10-11 *That ye might walk worthy of the Lord unto all pleasing, being fruitful in every good work, and increasing in the knowledge of God; Strengthened with all might, according to his glorious power, unto all patience and longsuffering with joyfulness;*

JEALOUS HEART

One wants what another has
to have as their very own
They don't want to see you with it
no matter what was sown

They try and try to do what another has done
of course without very much success
Even seeking praise from others
as being the very best

Stop looking at others with jealousy
ask God to cleanse your heart
Let the Spirit of God lead you
He will make your way clear, setting you apart

You can then be proud of who God made you to be
and content with what He supplies
Stop looking at what you don't have
to see your own blessings, just open up your eyes

PRAYER: Lord, where there are feelings of jealousy in me, cleanse it and help me to be content with how you have blessed me. Let me see all your rich gifts that you shower upon me daily as your way of getting me to where you want me to be. Help me to know without a doubt that what you do for me is fashioned just for me and for my best interest. Let your will always be done in my life. This I pray, in Jesus' name, amen.

WORRY

Worry: verb worried, worrying. - to torment oneself with or suffer from disturbing thoughts; to fret.

We must realize that if we are children of God we are not the captains of our own souls— as the saying goes. It is God who is in control. So, when our minds start to dwell on the things that we cannot control, we enter into the worry-zone, the future zone; and future things belong to God alone. Yes, there are things that we can manage in our lives but those things that matter the most are controlled by our God, our maker. Worry tells God that we don't trust Him to handle whatever situation we find ourselves in. God has promised to never leave or forsake us, Hebrews 13:5. We must trust that He is right there with us as He has promised. Doing so is what will help us to get through situations without coming apart at the seams. When the child of God yields to God's capable management of their life, they are saying, "God I trust you because I know you know what is best for me."

The scriptures tell us not to worry about what we are going to eat, drink or wear (Matthew 6:25-31). Remember, we are made in the image of God and are surely worth more than grass and birds. Don't worry about anything, instead pray about everything. Although He already knows, tell God what you need, and thank Him for what He has already done for you. Most of the things that we let worry us will never happen. They are mostly stretches of our own imaginations.

(Don't worry – Trust God)

PRAYER: Lord, show me your ways. Teach me your paths. Guide me in your truth and teach me, for you are God my Savior and my hope is in you all day long. (Psalms 24:4-5 NIV)

THOUGHT: We can if we will, turn our worry into hope when we focus on God our Father as Provider. It very well could be for our own good that we encounter the challenges we face. For most opportunities to trust God come from difficulties.

Psalms 77:2-3; 10-11 "The Psalmist was facing a difficult situation that vexed him and he thought there was no comfort for him. However, he turned his thoughts to God instead of on his dilemma. He remembered the goodness of God and changed his focus from worry to worship, from worry to hope, which led him to thanking God for what He had done in the past."

When we remember the goodness of God and how He worked in the lives of others, we can rest assured He is faithful to do the same for us.

FROM WORRY TO WORSHIP

Frazzled by the things that happen
Will leave you in a fix
Letting each distraction
Hit you like a ton of bricks

Taking your eyes totally off God
And all He wants to be to you
Making it seem that you were all alone
Facing the world, not knowing what to do

Stop. Seek God's presence
You will find His love and peace therein
Hope and confidence will help you see your way
To trusting God again

Worship will overtake concerns you may have
Just you wait and see
Keep your mind on your Father
And watch your worries flee

Know in your heart that
Worship is a privilege every believer holds
By it you celebrate the care and protection
God's Love for you enfolds

PRIDE

Pride: noun - a high or inordinate opinion of one's own dignity, importance, merit, or superiority, whether as cherished in the mind or as displayed in conduct.

Pride can also be defined as having too much belief in yourself. It causes disappointments, prevents growth, and leaves us stagnated. Pride gives us a false sense of accomplishment. We start to believe we have arrived, attained, but in truth we have not. When in reality we are stuck in a place of emptiness that produces nothing but heartache and false hope. We shut down the learning process and we close our ears to listening. Pride prevents us from looking at new ways of thinking and doing. These new ways are found in the Word of God. They are instructions designed to renew our minds, if we only allow it.

Soon pride causes us to close ourselves off to others' opinions. We become unteachable, unreachable and unaffected by even the voice of God. Are you teachable? Are you open to learning even in an area where you may be educated and skilled? Humble yourself and let the Lord lift you to new heights never imagined!

INSIGHT: Right in the middle of pride is "I."

PRIDE

FOR YOUR READING:
Proverbs 29:23 *A man's pride shall bring him low: but honour shall uphold the humble in spirit.*

Proverbs 11:2 *When pride cometh, then cometh shame: but with the lowly is wisdom.*

Proverbs 13:10 *Only by pride cometh contention: but with the well advised is wisdom.*

Proverbs 16:18 *Pride goeth before destruction, and an haughty spirit before a fall.*

I John 2:16 *For all that is in the world, the lust of the flesh, and the lust of the eyes, and the pride of life, is not of the Father, but is of the world.*

PRAYER: Lord teach me to be humble in all I say and do. Amen.

ANGER

Anger: noun - a strong feeling of displeasure and belligerence aroused by a wrong; wrath;

Anger is profoundly a self-serving emotion. It usually worsens every situation involving it. It reduces every relationship to a battle ground, and places one as dominate over the other. Anger destroys civility and promotes bitterness. It leads to sadness, and sadness leads to feelings of loneliness, abandonment, and worst. It causes us to respond in unfavorable ways. Anger wants to be heard. It wants to be justified. What causes you to become angry, never equals the fury or fierceness it expels, and causes you to overreact in most situations.

Anger, some say, is a pressure cooker, which explodes with time because it ignores one's self-monitoring ability. In most cases, it will not be denied because of selfish roots. We insist on being right. Rationale is tossed aside and confusion is dominate and will not be opposed by rational advice.

Anger can be expressed in many ways; in body language, loud words, aggression, and retaliation, to name a few. It is usually a warning to those who are the objects of it—warning them of coming retaliation. Anger is a defense mechanism, but is best served when it is used to ward off undesirable outcomes. Anger impairs one's ability to control behavior. Finally, anger is a manipulative bully that should be avoided whenever possible.

I am reminded of the story of Jonah. It holds an important life lesson we can all benefit from. After he finally did what God wanted him to do—which was to preach to the people of Nineveh about turning from their wicked ways, and back to God. When the people heard the warning preached by Jonah, they obeyed, but this angered Jonah. He was displeased with their obedience and God's mercy towards them. His anger caused him to not want God to pardon them?

Clearly, his anger was unfounded, and unnecessary. Anger always flaws one's reasoning. Only a change of heart and mind can free such thinking.

PRAYER: Lord, help us to not allow our emotions to cloud our thinking and cause us to do or say anything that will be a hindrance to our being the righteous people you want us to be. In Jesus' name, amen.

THOUGHT: "A heart filled with anger has no room for love."~ Unknown

UNGRATEFULNESS

Ungratefulness: noun – lack of gratitude, thanklessness.

If there were degrees to the enemies of the blessings of righteousness, ungratefulness would be right there close to the top of the list. Ingratitude reeks of a hardened heart.

Let us not think that just because the fourth Thursday in November has been set aside to give thanks for all our blessings that it is enough. We must develop and practice thankfulness to God every day because He is good every day. We can never thank God enough for all His benefits to us. Don't get me wrong, Thanksgiving is a beautiful day and one of my favorite holidays. It is a special day to enjoy being together with family and friends, preparing good food to enjoy and calling attention to what we are thankful to God for.

The reason ungratefulness develops in some of us is because we hear things like, "God knows your heart"; "He knows you love Him and thank Him." This is what the enemy wants us to believe so that we don't think it is necessary to tell God what He already knows. Believe me, God wants to hear from us how much we appreciate what He does for us. The more we are given the more we must thank God. Not only thank Him but have a grateful attitude that shows up in other parts of our lives. Sharing with others who are less fortunate, willingly operating in our gifts, and telling others about the goodness of God are all perfect ways to show God we are grateful for His blessings to us.

At the opposite end of blessings are troubles and hardships. When we experience one trouble after another in our lives, we would be wise not to allow them to cause us to become ungrateful towards God. Even in our troubles, God is faithful. He is always with His children to lead them and guide them in and through whatever comes upon them. Just because we are experiencing lean times does not mean that God is not good to us, or, that He has abandoned us. Hardships have a way of making us strong when we are delivered from them; but only when we know that it was God who kept us and delivered us. You must know that ungratefulness tells God that we don't trust Him to see us through our troubles, or that what we have we achieved on our own.

The more we have, the more thankful we should be. But closer to the truth is that those who are given more are often the least grateful and those who have less are often the most grateful. Take a look at Luke 17:11-19 at the 10 lepers Jesus healed of leprosy. Only one came back to say "thank you." The nine took their blessing and went on about their way not even acknowledging Jesus and what He had done for them. Don't be guilty of being in "the nine", be the one who lets God know how grateful you are, every day, for every blessing He bestows. He is worthy to be praised.

God is ever at work in the lives of His people, blessing them in ways only He can. That thought alone should be reason enough to be grateful. Now think of all the unseen things God is doing in and through the lives of His people. He is healing bodies, ordering steps and redirecting paths, charting destinies, working miracles and delivering us from destruction.

Gratitude is a sign of maturity. Praying to God should never consist of just asking for things. It also involves letting Him know we are grateful for the blessings we have already received. Start a "Gratitude Journal" today and see just how many blessings you can name.

PRAYER: Help us to be grateful people. Search our hearts and remove every element that would cause us to be ungrateful. Thank you for your love, amen.

THOUGHT: Learning to say "Thank You" would be a great use of our time. It is as important to the believer as breathing.

THANK YOU

Thank you Lord for your love and kindness
shown to me always
For peace and joy, for health and strength
and for length of days

Fearfully and wondrously strong is how
you fashioned me
With many gifts and talents,
eternally thankful I'll be

It is by your mercy that I am able
this wonderful life to live
It's by your love and grace and multitude
of blessings that you give

Thanks for sending Jesus
to fulfill your glorious plan
To shed light in the darkness and
redeem fallen man

For sin was so rampant and
lives were so lost
But, Christ went about to reconcile us
with no fear of the cost

I know that you love me because
your Word tells me so
And it is by that very love
you hold me and never let me go

Yes, it must have been that very love
that kept Christ on that tree
Suffering for sins He did not commit
just to set the captives free

So thank you Lord for your love
and kindness shown to me always
For peace and joy, for health and strength
and for length of days

WE HAVE SO VERY MUCH TO BE GRATEFUL FOR

FOR YOUR READING:

Psalm 100:4 *Enter into his gates with thanksgiving, and into his courts with praise: be thankful unto him, and bless his name.*

Psalm 139:14 *I will praise thee; for I am fearfully and wonderfully made: marvellous are thy works; and that my soul knoweth right well.*

Psalm 50:14 *Offer unto God thanksgiving; and pay thy vows unto the most High:*

BOASTFULNESS

Boastfulness: noun - 1. The act or an instance of bragging. 2. A source of pride.

Scripture shows us that God does not approve of boasters. Rather, He commands us to humble ourselves before Him. Boasting and self-praise steals the glory due only to God. It is a fact that God will not stand for sharing of His glory.

If you are ever going to boast, let it be in the Lord. We have a good example of sinful braggers in Scripture with the self-righteous Pharisees. Pride hinders people from seeing the truth and makes them think they are something other than what they truly are. It makes them think they are better than others. Having a boastful spirit turns people off, they would rather not be around you.

Everything we are and ever will be is because God has allowed it. He is the only one that deserves the praise for it. Don't get me wrong, having pride in who God has made us is not wrong. It only becomes wrong when we think we arrived there on our own.

Acts 17:28 says ~ For in him we live, and move, and have our being; as certain also of your own poets have said, "For we are also his offspring." So if we live and move and have our being in God, where then do we have the right to boast about anything? It is God's breath and by God's power that we are able to do anything. Thankfulness should flood our hearts that the God of the universe made it possible for us to live in Him.

I Corinthians 13:4-8 "Charity (Love) suffereth long, and is kind; charity envieth not; charity vaunteth (boasts) not itself, is not puffed up, Doth not behave itself unseemly, seeketh not her own, is not easily provoked, thinketh no evil; Rejoiceth not in iniquity, but rejoiceth in the truth; Beareth all things, believeth all things, hopeth all things, endureth all things. Charity never faileth: but whether there be prophecies, they shall fail; whether there be tongues, they shall cease; whether there be knowledge, it shall vanish away."

God is love and having love in our hearts for God and our fellowman will help us to not be boastful creatures. It is God who made us and not we ourselves. I will say it again, if we ever have occasion to boast, let it be "in the Lord." Be free to tell of God's goodness in your life. Tell of the blessings He has bestowed upon you. Boast of the distance he has brought the person you were (before you said yes to Him) to where you are now. Brag about the difference His love has made in your life, in your conversation and in your heart. Brag about what a good, great and awesome God He is. Now, that's worth bragging about!

THOUGHT: If God made you who you are, and gave you what you have, brought you where you are, and if God's is whose you are, then what right do you have to brag about any of it?

FOR YOUR READING:

Matthew 6:1-2 *Take heed that ye do not your alms before men, to be seen of them: otherwise ye have no reward of your Father which is in heaven.*

Proverbs 26:12 *Seest thou a man wise in his own conceit? more hope of a fool than of him.*

James 4:6 *But he giveth more grace. Wherefore he saith, God resisteth the proud, but giveth grace unto the humble.*

1 Samuel 2:3 *"Do not keep talking so proudly or let your mouth speak such arrogance, for the LORD is a God who knows, and by him deeds are weighed.*

Psalm 5:5 *The boastful shall not stand before your eyes; you hate all evildoers.*

Colossians 3:9 *Lie not one to another, seeing that ye have put off the old man with his deeds;*

Proverbs 12:16 *A fool's wrath is presently known: but a prudent [man] covereth shame.*

1 Corinthians 13:3 *If I give all I possess to the poor and give over my body to hardship that I may boast, but do not have love, I gain nothing.*

2 Timothy 3:1-5 *But mark this: There will be terrible times in the last days. People will be lovers of themselves, lovers of money, boastful, proud, abusive, disobedient to their parents, ungrateful, unholy, without love, unforgiving, slanderous, without self-control, brutal, not lovers of the good, treacherous, rash, conceited, lovers of pleasure rather than lovers of God having a form of godliness but denying its power. Have nothing to do with such people.*

Jude 1:16 *These people are grumblers and faultfinders; they follow their own evil desires; they boast about themselves and flatter others*

GREED

Greed: noun - 1. excessive consumption of or desire for food; gluttony 2. excessive desire, as for wealth or power.

The fifth deadly sin is greed. Greed is an inordinate love for money and possessions. Money and possessions are good gifts God gives to us. He allows us to be gainfully employed so we can take care of ourselves and our families financially. But greed is when we can't get enough and the pursuit of possessions consumes us. Wanting more overtakes you.

There are consequences that greed brings. It deadens us to the plights and needs of others around us. God gives us what he gives us so that we can provide for ourselves and our families along with helping others in their time of need. The more we are given, the more responsibility we have to support and care for others. "To whom much is given, much is required" Luke 12:48.

It is not just others who suffer as a consequence of our greed. We too face emotional challenges when we succumb to greed. There is never enough and we will always be left wanting more. If you are not content with what you have, believe me, you will not be content with more. No matter how much we store up for ourselves, there will always be things bigger and better and greed will make us want it. Greed causes us to miss out on the most satisfying things in life. Things like our true

51

calling in life, contributions to another's life that only you can supply, love you can share with the unloved, and ultimately having peace with, from and of God. All these treasured things we lose sight of as we pursue worldly wealth.

America is filled with greed. Our capitalistic and consumeristic economy is built on greed. We see greed all around us and yet we cannot help but get sucked in by it.

Jesus says we cannot serve two masters. We will be devoted to one and hate the other (Matthew 6:24). Greed will negatively affect our relationship with God. We may give God everything in our life but the last thing we often give is our checkbooks/money. Maybe this is the reason Jesus talked about money and possession so much in scripture. He knew the grip things would have on us, and that this would be a great stumbling block for many. My pastor's warning regarding this is "you have things, don't let things have you."

The virtue that stands in strictest opposition of greed is generosity. We serve a generous God and liberalgiving and sharing is born out of a relationship with him (James 1:5, Titus 3:5–6). There is a freedom that comes with generosity. Greed has us so blinded that we think that we own our money and possessions, but what often happens is our money and possessions own us. They start to control and dictate how we live.

If you are going to be greedy, be greedy for more and more of Jesus and His way.

GREED

G etting and wanting more than what is needed

R otten attitudes that spoil any situation

E verything has to go your way

E xpecting more of others than you are willing to give

D emanding it now

SELFISHNESS

Selfishness - noun - Concerned chiefly or only with oneself; stinginess resulting from a concern for your own welfare and a disregard of others; a lack of generosity; a general unwillingness to part with money, possessions.

Selfishness is at the very core of this world's moral breakdown. The mindless whims and desires of the selfish tramples over everyone and everything in sight when self-gratification is its goal. Nothing and nobody is important in the eyes of the selfish.

Selfish people are not concerned with the wishes of others, even when it is clear that the actions of such people will cause hurt and unhappiness to others. They trust no one but themselves and they love no one more than themselves. Nothing is ever enough to satisfy their self-centeredness.

The worldly doctrine says "do whatever you can to get what you want, don't hesitate to satisfy your needs, first." This is in strict contrast to what the Word of God teaches – putting others first. Putting others before yourself honors God. But be advised that doing this is not easy. It is not comfortable or natural. The natural instinct is to take care of self. Yet, as Christians, we believe we are given a new nature at salvation. Part of this nature is summed up in Galatians 6th chapter. The fruit of the Spirit is all about putting others before oneself.

Galatians 6:22,23 "But the fruit of the Spirit is love, joy, peace, longsuffering, gentleness, goodness, faith, meekness, temperance: against such there is no law."

One of the attributes that characterizes Christ is His compassion, His love, for He is love. Yes, He is God, but He was also a man with a desire to serve others because of His love for them. Since Jesus Christ is our example, we too should pray for a servant's heart and the right attitude if we don't already possess them. Serving is all but impossible without the Holy Spirit's help.

"You can love without serving, but you cannot serve without loving."

Ask God to develop compassion in your heart so that your serving will be done with the right attitude. Remember, He said to His followers that those who are truly His disciples will show love one to another.

Selfishness can spring up in many ways in our lives if we allow it to. Loving only fellow Christians and shunning all others who do not know our Father is one way. The example that Christ gave was of Him loving other people regardless of their spiritual condition. Try to put yourself in their situation and treat them as you would like to be treated. We call this the Golden Rule and it is found in Matthew 7:12. "Therefore all things whatsoever ye would that men should do to you, do ye even so to them: for this is the law and the prophets." Embrace this scripture and watch selfishness vanish.

FOR YOUR READING:

Philippians 2:3-4 *Let nothing be done through strife or vainglory; but in lowliness of mind let each esteem other better than themselves. Look not every man on his own things, but every man also on the things of others.*

I John 3:17 *But whoso hath this world's good, and seeth his brother have need, and shutteth up his bowels of compassion from him, how dwelleth the love of God in him?*

I Corinthians 10:24 *Let no man seek his own, but every man another's wealth.*

Galatians 6:2 *Bear ye one another's burdens, and so fulfill the law of Christ.*

James 3:16-18 *For where envying and strife is, there is confusion and every evil work. But the wisdom that is from above is first pure, then peaceable, gentle, and easy to be intreated, full of mercy and good fruits, without partiality, and without hypocrisy. And the fruit of righteousness is sown in peace, of them that make peace.*

Romans 8:5-9 *For they that are after the flesh do mind the things of the flesh; but they that are after the Spirit the things of the Spirit. For to be carnally minded is death; but to be spiritually minded is life and peace. Because the carnal mind is enmity against God: for it is not subject to* *the law of God, neither indeed can be. So then they that are in the flesh cannot please God. But ye are not in the flesh, but in the Spirit, if so be that the Spirit of God dwell in you. Now if any man have not the Spirit of Christ, he is none of his.*

II Corinthians 5:15 *And that he died for all, that they which live should not henceforth live unto themselves, but unto him which died for them, and rose again.*

Proverbs 18:1 *Through desire a man, having separated himself, seeketh and intermeddleth (searches for a quarrel) with all wisdom.*

Romans 2:6-9 *Who will render to every man according to his deeds: To them who by patient continuance in well doing seek for glory and honour and immortality, eternal life: But unto them that are contentious (selfish), and do not obey the truth, but obey unrighteousness, indignation and wrath, tribulation and anguish, upon every soul of man that doeth evil, of the Jew first, and also of the Gentile;*

Philippians 2:2-3 *Fulfil ye my joy, that ye be likeminded, having the same love, being of one accord, of one mind. Let nothing be done through strife (selfishness) or vainglory (evil conceit); but in lowliness of mind let each esteem other better than themselves.*

SELFISH
(*as defined by my pastor, John H. Brown*)

Get all you can
Can all you get
Then, sit on the can

SELFISHNESS

I'm gonna get everything I can
While I can
Whenever I can
For as long as I can

For me and only me
Because it is all about me
No one else matters, you see
I think of nobody but me

I work hard to gain all that I gain,
Then I store it far out of sight
To enjoy it myself, I hardly dare
But no one else will ever share

It is mine
All mine
For me, for me, for me
For I am SELFISHNESS, you see

A Google search revealed that John Wesley once said, "Get all you can, save all you can, give all you can."

This attitude is closer to the way God wants us to be. Being selfish demeans the life God wants the believer to live. Taking what He allows us to gain and using it for our enjoyment as well as sharing with others. This shows God's love to those who are without His goodness, favor and salvation. Never let selfishness be the badge you wear for others to see. Our God is good and gracious - our example to follow.

Matthew 22:39 "And the second is like unto it, Thou shalt love thy neighbour as thyself."

WARNING: Don't let Selfishness be the position you take or the condition of your heart.

SLOTHFULNESS

Slothfulness (laziness): adjective - Disinclined to work or exertion; lazy.

Slothfulness is associated with laziness and a lack of energy. Sloths, the mammals of South and Central America, are called such because of their slow movements. We commonly associate someone who is slothful as someone who is vegged out on the couch and unable to engage themselves in any meaningful way. But when it comes to slothfulness as a deadly sin, there is more to it than a lack of energy.

This enemy of the blessings of righteousness is more about priorities than it is about energy. Slothfulness is failing to pour our energy into the things that really matter. Like spending quality time with our Maker, families, and friends. When we brag to one another about how busy we are at any given time, the problem may be that we are busy with all the wrong things. It leaves us filled with stress and anxiety which are hindrances to our relationship with God and our fellowman. When we allow things to get in the way of us nurturing our time with God and our families we can be left filled with great regret.

Always rushing to the urgent, unimportant things, we may never get to the real important things in our lives. We miss out on the things that are the most fulfilling.

Undeniably we need "down time", but we equally need time with God and our families. Down time is watching TV, playing video games, listening to music, shopping, watching sports, and entertainment, and hobbies. When we let these things and things like them become our unyielding passion, we forfeit times of importance that can be spent with our loved ones or quiet time seeking God's presence with a desire to know Him better.

Think about the passion many people have for their favorite sports team. Just imagine the amazing things that would happen if we had that same passion for God.

The virtue of obedience is what stands in opposition to slothfulness; and obedience is about priority and purpose. The reason some people don't make their purpose a priority is because they don't know their purpose. A Christian's purpose is to love God with all their heart and soul and love others as they love themselves (Matthew 22:38-39). They live aimless lives failing to engage in what is truly important. Do you live your life on purpose? And, is that purpose in line with God's plan for you? Or, are you living without any goal or mission in life? We will forever fall victim to the things that don't really matter if we live our lives apart from what God designed it to be.

Let's look at Jesus, our Savior's, life. He lived his life on a mission and on purpose. It was to save the world from their sin. Many things happened that could have distracted him from His mission, but His sole focus was to do the will of the Father and to complete His mission.

Yes, there are emails, posts to Facebook, text messages, and voicemails screaming for your attention. There is a house to clean and lawn to be mowed, diapers to change and laundry to be washed. There are groceries to be bought and meals to be cooked, closets to be cleaned, and beds to be made, books to be read and books to be written. There are miles to be driven and new things to see and experience. Life will always be filled with urgent and not-so-urgent matters, but the question still remains — will you allow any of these or other things to distract you from the REAL important things in life —God, family, others?

FOR YOUR READING:
Proverbs 6:6 *Go to the ant, thou sluggard; consider her ways, and be wise:*

Proverbs 19:15 *Slothfulness casteth into a deep sleep; and an idle soul shall suffer hunger.*

Colossians 3:23 *And whatsoever ye do, do [it] heartily, as to the Lord, and not unto men;*

Ecclesiastes 10:18 *By much slothfulness the building decayeth; and through idleness of the hands the house droppeth through.*

Proverbs 21:25 *The desire of the slothful killeth him; for his hands refuse to labour.*

THOUGHT: Slothfulness hinders a man from being the husband and father his wife and children need him to be. It keeps the woman from being the wife and mother she needs to be and blocks the children from becoming the God-fearing and obedient children they need to be. Everyone is hinderened by slothfulness.

PRAYER: Lord give us the desire to seek your presence daily. Help us to know our purpose and help us to live every day fulfilling it. When we become distracted by laziness, encourage us to return to the things that really matter. In Jesus' name.

SLANDER

Slander: noun - Oral communication of false statements injurious to a person's reputation. 2. A false and malicious statement or report about someone.

Matthew 5:11"Blessed are ye, when men shall revile you, and persecute you, and shall say all manner of evil against you falsely, for my sake."

I Peter 3:14-17 "But sanctify the Lord God in your hearts: and be ready always to give an answer to every man that asketh you a reason of the hope that is in you with meekness and fear: Having a good conscience; that, whereas they speak evil of you, as of evildoers, they may be ashamed that falsely accuse your good conversation in Christ. For it is better, if the will of God be so, that ye suffer for well doing, than for evil doing."

You are blessed when you suffer for the sake of Christ. If you are living by God's precepts and teachings, you are a good candidate for being slandered by those allowing the enemy to use them in such a way.

Slander is one of the tools used to cause division and strife among friends.

One of my pastor's sayings is "It's okay to be blamed for something, just be less the blame." That means no matter what slanderous accusation someone lodges against you, fear not, if it is false. It may cause pain and discomfort for a season but the truth will surface. And when it does the accuser will suffer shame, not you.

Slander has no place in the life of the believer. The Bible teaches that we are to uplift and edify each other. When we are the victim of false accusations, it causes suffering. We as believers will do well to be on the right side of this suffering by making sure you are not the one causing it.

People who slander another's good behavior in Christ have no peace in their life. What is worse, they resent you for having and exhibiting peace in yours.

The Bible says in Proverbs - "the man who speaks a slander upon another is a fool. " I don't know about you, but I don't want to be guilty of being a fool or suffering the loss of blessings God has in store for me.

Living a righteous life has no room for slanderous activity. When we live obediently to God's word, we set ourselves up to be blessed by God.

FOR YOUR READING:

Romans 14:17-19 *For the kingdom of God is not meat and drink; but righteousness, and peace, and joy in the Holy Ghost. For he that in these things serveth Christ is acceptable to God, and approved of men. Let us therefore follow after the things which make for peace, and things wherewith one may edify another.*

I Corinthians 10:23 *All things are lawful for me, but all things are not expedient: all things are lawful for me, but all things edify not.*

I Thessalonians 5:11 *Wherefore comfort yourselves together, and edify one another, even as also ye do.*

Proverbs 10:18 *He that hideth hatred with lying lips, and he that uttereth a slander, is a fool.*

PREJUDICE

Prejudice: noun - 1. An adverse judgment or opinion formed beforehand or without knowledge or examination of the facts. A preconceived preference or idea. 2. The act or state of holding unreasonable preconceived judgments or convictions.

Prejudice packs with it maliciousness. It is void of proof or evidence in any given situation because it is based on what seems valid in the mind of the perpetrator. He/she has set themself as "judge." The Bible tells us that there is only one true judge, God.

Our thoughts and attitudes govern our prejudices. Prejudice evolves into discrimination when we act on those thoughts and attitudes. When we make assumptions about someone we cause unfairness in the way they are preceived by others. Even if that person is an unbeliever, God loves them. It is hard enough to witness to people who are different from us, but how much more difficult would it be if we harbor prejudice against them? God wants us to love people, not alienate ourselves from them.

Where God's people are concerned, they are warned to love one another as Christ loved them. (I John 3:11; John 15:12; 17; John 13:34-35).

People are different. They think differently. They have different likes and dislikes. They look different, they dress differently. People even worship God differently. There is only one God and if you worship Him in spirit and in truth you will be rewarded. For that is what God expects from us. (John 4:24)

When we stop grouping ourselves according to our differences and start working together despite our differences, we will get more done to expand the Kingdom of our God on this earth, which is what God wants us to do. (Mark 16:15)

PRAYER: Lord, help us, your children, to work together in harmony and with gratitude for your gift of salvation. Thank you for giving us this wonderful opportunity to love and serve one another. Help us to love the world enough to tell them about your goodness so that they too can be numbered among your people. Amen.

THOUGHT: Prejudice separates, while love includes. It alienates, love reconciles, and prejudice darkens, but love enlightens and illuminates. There is never room for prejudice among the body of Christ.

FOR YOUR READING:

Romans 14:13 *Let us not therefore judge one another any more: but judge this rather, that no man put a stumbling block or an occasion to fall in his brother's way.*

I Corinthians 6:5 *I speak to your shame. Is it so, that there is not a wise man among you? no, not one that shall be able to judge between his brethren?*

Ezekiel 18:30 *Therefore I will judge you, O house of Israel, every one according to his ways, saith the Lord GOD. Repent, and turn yourselves from all your transgressions; so iniquity shall not be your ruin.*

Psalms 75:7 *But God is the judge: he putteth down one, and setteth up another.*

Matthew 7:1 *Judge not, that ye be not judged.*

HAUGHTINESS

Haughtiness: noun - To act in an aloof, snobbish, or condescending manner.

Haughtiness is first cousin to pride. Having a haughty spirit causes one to be arrogant and conceited. They have a tendency to think more of themselves than they ought. "If I were you, I would want to be me", is the attitude taken by most high-minded people. This is something the Bible warns us of. (Romans 12:3) A haughty spirit is one of the six things that God hates. (Proverbs 21:4)

Looking down on people who are different with disdain and disgust rather than as human beings, made in the image of God is their specialty. They let their arrogance rule them so that snobbery, superiority and self-importance shines brightly in their behavior.

The opposite of haughtiness is humbleness. Being humble is what the Lord expects from His people. When we are humble we realize that it is God who made us who we are. We would be nothing without Him and we could do nothing without His help. He made us to love and worship Him. He even gave us a blueprint, the Bible, to be able to live righteous lives.

The haughty person sets himself above others, and at the end of the day, above God himself. He becomes the center or focus of his own world; everything and everybody revolves around him. Another's opinion is of no concern to him. He even shows no consideration where the will of God is concerned. This is why there is no regard for others or God, and there is nothing off limits or unlawful to him.

God sees haughtiness as an enemy to the blessings He wants to bestow upon the righteous. It is mentioned over and over in both the Old and New Testament scriptures that God brings down the haughty and the proud. (Psalm 18:27; Isaiah 2:11, 5:15; Ezekiel 16:50, Proverbs 16:18, 18:12; James 4:6;1 Peter 5:5).

When you recognize you are too high-minded, you must humble yourself and ask God for forgiveness. Then you can serve God in the spirit of meekness, love and humility.

PRAYER: Lord, give us clean hearts and humble spirits so that we may follow you with our whole hearts. Help us to treat others as we ourselves would like to be treated. Help us to know that you have no respect of persons and neither should we. Because haughtiness precedes destruction, help us to be humble, caring people as you have exampled before us. In Jesus' name, amen.

FOR YOUR READING:

I Corinthians 4:7 *For who maketh thee to differ from another? and what hast thou that thou didst not receive? now if thou didst receive it, why dost thou glory, as if thou hadst not received it?*

Isaiah 66:1-2 *Thus saith the LORD, The heaven is my throne, and the earth is my footstool: where is the house that ye build unto me? and where is the place of my rest? For all those things hath mine hand made, and all those things have been, saith the LORD: but to this man will I look, even to him that is poor and of a contrite spirit, and trembleth at my word.*

FILTHY COMMUNICATION

Filthy Communications: adjective - characterized by or full of filth; very dirty or obscene, unpleasant, vile   2. offensive or vicious

It is bad for one to have filthy thoughts. It is really bad when those thoughts are verbalized. But either way, thought or spoken words, God knows. The Word of God reminds us in Matthew 15:18-19 of what pollutes a person. Words from the mouth are straight from the heart and they will either defile or edify.

Only you determine which you will speak. It is a choice that each of us has to make as to what we allow to come out of our mouths. Usually, if the heart is corrupt, the speech will be too. We must guard our hearts against things that will damage our witness and sabotage us from being right with God.

When we become children of God it is incumbent upon each of us to allow the Holy Spirit of God to rule our very being. That includes what we say, do, think and how we behave. We must not forget that we are representatives of Christ. We have watchers everywhere we go. What will your "watchers" see in you? What will they hear you speak?

Vulgarity is an intense form of language that undermines or weakens our relationship with Christ. Because what we speak is a direct product of the heart, we need to ask God to give us clean hearts so that we can only speak those things that are pleasing to Him. A less intense form of language is to revile, insult or berate. All these are harmful to the person it is aimed at and harmful to the character of the person saying it. An example of this is the surprising ease of words spoken when a person cuts us off in traffic. Further examples are: "giving them a piece of your mind", "giving someone a "tongue lashing", and resorting to name calling ("Idiot! Dummy! Moron!", etc.).

A father knows what his child needs. If God is your father, ask Him to bridle your tongue so that you only speak wholesome words that edify and uplift, that encourage and inspire. This is not an impossible task. Ask God and be ready to change.

FOR YOUR READING:

Psalms 39:1 *I said, I will take heed to my ways, that I sin not with my tongue: I will keep my mouth with a bridle, while the wicked is before me.*

Colossians 3:8 *But now ye also put off all these; anger, wrath, malice, blasphemy, filthy communication out of your mouth.*

James 3:2 *For in many things we offend all. If any man offend not in word, the same is a perfect man, and able also to bridle the whole body.*

Philippians 4:6-8 *Be careful for nothing; but in everything by prayer and supplication with thanksgiving let your requests be made known unto God. And the peace of God, which passeth all understanding, shall keep your hearts and minds through Christ Jesus. Finally, brethren, whatsoever things are true, whatsoever things are honest, whatsoever things are just, whatsoever things are pure, whatsoever things are lovely, whatsoever things are of good report; if there be any virtue, and if there be any praise, think on these things.*

PRAYER: Thank you Father that you give us a new heart and a new life when we come to you for forgiveness, confessing our sins. Help us to live a life that reflects your great gift of salvation. May our lives be monuments of a life lived for you, and guided by your Spirit. May others see what a difference you have made in us. May this difference inspire them to follow you wholly in their lives. In Jesus' Precious Name. Amen.

THOUGHT: Guard your heart, (Proverbs 4:23-24) "for everything you do flows from it. Keep thy heart with all diligence; for out of it are the issues of life. Put away from thee a froward mouth, and perverse lips put far from thee."

BITTERNESS

Bitterness: adjective - Proceeding from or exhibiting strong animosity. Resulting from, or expressive severe grief, anguish, or disappointment. Marked by resentment or cynicism.

There are many reasons people become bitter; abandonment, loneliness, disownment, aloneness, and desertion are just a few.

It is a fact that smoking, drinking, and unhealthy eating are the causes of many illnesses and diseases. But more and more of our physical sicknesses are the result of our spiritual condition. Many people are sick with bitterness. They are resentful and angry as time passes and their bitterness takes root. Then it grows within them and manifests through physical illness and other ailments. These physical illnesses can be treated with various medications, but there is nothing to treat bitterness.

Holding on to bitterness is so detrimental to spiritual growth in the believer and it is a hindrance to receiving Christ into the life of a non-believer. You must not nurture bitter feelings because the only one to suffer hurt from it is you.

Bitterness will make you sick. The scriptures tell us in Hebrews 12:15 "the 'root of bitterness' springs up and causes trouble."

Did you know that bitterness is a tool of the devil

that he uses to destroy relationships? It imprisons us in isolation and prevents us from experiencing the healing we so desperately need from God. Do all you can to detach yourself from bitterness. There is nothing good that can ever come from holding on to it. Nothing!

Bitterness is on open display in our world. It can be seen between rival political parties, splits and divisions in the church and in nations. We see bitterness in families, marriages, and friendships. It just seems that it is the popular choice to take when we are dealt undesirable situations in our lives. When this bitterness route is taken, we forfeit the opportunity to be reconciled.

Let me warn you, "bitterness is not easy to let go of. You can't do it on your own." You can only do it through the strength and power that God gives you through Jesus Christ and The Holy Spirit of God. Start by asking God to forgive you for allowing bitterness to reside in your heart. Read God's word to see what it says about it. Then go forth doing all you can do to walk pleasing to God with a heart open to love—to be able to love God, others, and yourself.

REMEMBER: Jesus had every right to be bitter but He chose to love instead. Among the reasons He could have been bitter are:
- toward Judas for betraying Him
- toward the other disciples for deserting Him
- toward the religious leaders for accusing Him of wrongdoing

- toward us for not seeing and recognizing the magnitude of His sacrifice on the cross, but instead of being bitter He chose to die for all the world.

Upon the cross, Christ was given the bitter wine vinegar to drink (Matthew 27:48) He physically tasted the bitterness of the vinegar, but "Praise God" bitter was the opposite of what he chose to be. He chose love. He chose to die for the sins of the world and through his blood he made provision for the forgiveness of all the ways we ever offended him.

You may have a right to be bitter and angry about an offense you may have been dealt, but letting Christ do a new thing in you will help you once again taste the sweetness of Jesus! When you allow Him to soften your heart, you choose His way that is opposite of bitterness. Choose love. Choose Jesus' way.

FOR YOUR READING:

Matthew 6:12-15 *And forgive us our debts, as we forgive our debtors. And lead us not into temptation, but deliver us from evil: For thine is the kingdom, and the power, and the glory, for ever. Amen. For if ye forgive men their trespasses, your heavenly Father will also forgive you: But if ye forgive not men their trespasses, neither will your Father forgive your trespasses.*

Hebrews 12:12-17 *Wherefore lift up the hands which hang down, and the feeble knees; And make straight paths for your feet, lest that which is lame be turned out of the way; but let it rather be healed. Follow peace with all men, and holiness, without which no man shall see the Lord: Looking diligently lest any man fail of the grace of God; lest any root of bitterness springing up trouble you, and thereby many be defiled; Lest there be any fornicator, or profane person, as Esau, who for one morsel of meat sold his birthright. For ye know how that afterward, when he would have inherited the blessing, he was rejected: for he found no place of repentance, though he sought it carefully with tears.*

Luke 15:25-32 *Now his elder son was in the field: and as he came and drew nigh to the house, he heard musick and dancing. And he called one of the servants, and asked what these things meant. And he said unto him, Thy brother is come; and thy father hath killed the fatted calf, because he hath received him safe and sound. And he was angry, and would not go in: therefore came his father out, and intreated him. And he answering said to his father, Lo, these many years do I serve thee, neither transgressed I at any time thy commandment: and yet thou never gavest me a kid, that I might make merry with my friends: But as soon as this thy son was come, which hath devoured thy living with harlots, thou hast killed for him the fatted calf. And he said unto him, Son, thou art ever with me, and all that I have is thine. It was meet that we should make merry, and be glad: for this thy brother was dead, and is alive again; and was lost, and is found.*

PRAYER: *Lord teach us to be loving, forgiving and seekers of your grace. When we feel that we have been wronged, help us to turn to you for guidance. Restore our peace and allow it to steer our hearts away from bitterness and the debilitating effects it brings. Destroy every root of bitterness that seeks to destroy us. Let us live so your name is glorified. In the name of Jesus, amen.*

EXCUSES

Excuse: verb (tr). to pardon or forgive, to seek pardon or exemption for, to excuse oneself for one's mistakes, to make allowances for; judge leniently: to excuse someone's ignorance, to serve as an apology or explanation for; vindicate or justify.

It would be very safe to say "nearly everyone is guilty of making an excuse at one time or another." An excuse is an unjustified or false reason for not doing something. It is usually given to mask the real reason. No excuse, is good enough to escape doing the will of God, especially if you happen to be a believer. If God asks you to do something, He knows you are equipped to do it. He has already placed in you what it will take to get the job done. God does not make mistakes, people do.

Excuse making is very old and very common. It started with the first man and woman, Adam and Eve in Genesis 3:9-13 and has continued until today. When we know to do the right thing and violate it by doing just the opposite, we are forfeiting a blessing that God wants to bestow upon us. In God's sight, we are without excuse.

Many times blame is cast upon others for our mistakes to divert the blame and responsibility from us. Romans 1:17-20 "For therein is the righteousness of God revealed from faith to faith: as it is written, the just shall live by faith. For the wrath of God is revealed from heaven against all ungodliness and unrighteousness of men, who hold the truth in unrighteousness; Because that which may be known of God is manifest in them; for God hath shewed it unto them. For the invisible things of him from the creation of the world are clearly seen, being understood by the things that are made, even his eternal power and Godhead; so that they are without excuse."

INSIGHT: No excuse is good enough to avoid doing the will of God. Some of the most common excuses are:

- I didn't feel well.
- I was real busy and couldn't get there.
- I had company visiting.
- I'm too old or too young.
- The messages aren't interesting to me.
- I'm not getting anything out of it.
- The weather was bad.
- There's too many hypocrites in the Church.
- I am not worthy.
- I can't speak like Mary Jane, and so on.

REMEMBER: God wants to use you to glorify Him and bless others. Trust Him that He knows what He is doing by asking you to do a specific task. He can use you despite any excuse you can come up with.

PRAYER: Lord, help us to not make excuses when we are given a task to do, whatever it may be. Let us realize that you have already equipped us to complete it. Let our motives be pure, our hearts be open and our spirits be free to obeying your every command. In Jesus' name, amen.

FOR YOUR READING:

Exodus 3:11-12 *And Moses said unto God, Who am I, that I should go unto Pharaoh, and that I should bring forth the children of Israel out of Egypt? And he said, Certainly I will be with thee; and this shall be a token unto thee, that I have sent thee: When thou hast brought forth the people out of Egypt, ye shall serve God upon this mountain.*

Exodus 4:10-12 *And Moses said unto the LORD, O my LORD, I am not eloquent, neither heretofore, nor since thou hast spoken unto thy servant: but I am slow of speech, and of a slow tongue. And the LORD said unto him, Who hath made man's mouth? or who maketh the dumb, or deaf, or the seeing, or the blind? have not I the LORD? Now therefore go, and I will be with thy mouth, and teach thee what thou shalt say.*

Judges 6:15-16 *And he said unto him, Oh my Lord, wherewith shall I save Israel? behold, my family is poor in Manasseh, and I am the least in my father's house. And the LORD said unto him, Surely I will be with thee, and* *thou shalt smite the Midianites as one man.*

Proverbs 26:13 *The sluggard says, "There is a lion outside; I will be killed in the streets.*

Jeremiah 1:6-8 *Then said I, Ah, Lord GOD! behold, I cannot speak: for I am a child. But the LORD said unto me, Say not, I am a child: for thou shalt go to all that I shall send thee, and whatsoever I command thee thou shalt speak. Be not afraid of their faces: for I am with thee to deliver thee, saith the LORD.*

Matthew 25:24-30 *Then he which had received the one talent came and said, Lord, I knew thee that thou art an hard man, reaping where thou hast not sown, and gathering where thou hast not strawed: And I was afraid, and went and hid thy talent in the earth: lo, there thou hast that is thine. His lord answered and said unto him, Thou wicked and slothful servant, thou knewest that I reap where I sowed not, and gather where I have not strawed: Thou oughtest therefore to have put my money to the exchangers, and then at my coming I should have received mine own with usury. Take therefore the talent from him, and give it unto him which hath ten talents. For unto every one that hath shall be given, and he shall have abundance: but from him that hath not shall be taken away even that which he hath. And cast ye the unprofitable servant into outer darkness: there shall be weeping and gnashing of teeth.*

Luke 14:16-24 *Then said he unto him, A certain man made a great supper, and bade many: And sent his servant at supper time to say to them that were bidden, Come; for all things are now ready. And they all with one consent began to make excuse. The first said unto him, I have bought a piece of ground, and I must needs go and see it: I pray thee have me excused. And another said, I have bought five yoke of oxen, and I go to prove them: I pray thee have me excused. And another said, I have married a wife, and therefore I cannot come. So that servant came, and shewed his lord these things. Then the master of the house being angry said to his servant, Go out quickly into the streets and lanes of the city, and bring in hither the poor, and the maimed, and the halt, and the blind. And the servant said, Lord, it is done as thou hast commanded, and yet there is room. And the lord said unto the servant, Go out into the highways and hedges, and compel them to come in, that my house may be filled. For I say unto you, That none of those men which were bidden shall taste of my supper.*

Luke 9:59-62 *And he said unto another, Follow me. But he said, Lord, suffer me first to go and bury my father. esus said unto him, Let the dead bury their dead: but go thou and preach the kingdom of God. And another also said, Lord, I will follow thee; but let me first go bid them farewell, which are at home at my house. And Jesus said unto him, No man, having put his hand to the plough, and looking back, is fit for the kingdom of God.*

EPILOGUE

It is impossible for one to live a righteous life apart from a relationship with God. Therefore, it is crucial to accept God's salvation through Jesus Christ, His son and begin to walk daily with Him. Maintaining a good relationship is nothing short of knowing what the Word of God says and doing it, no matter what your flesh tells you to do.

SO NOW, since we have been made right in God's sight by faith in His promises, we can have real peace with Him because of what Jesus Christ, our Lord, has done for us on the cross. Because of our faith, He has brought us into this place of highest privilege where we now stand. We confidently and joyfully look forward to becoming all God wants us to be. We can rejoice too, when we run into problems and trials, for we know that they are good for us. They help us to learn to be patient. And patience develops strength of character in us and helps us to trust God more each time we exercise our faith in Him. Finally, our hope and faith becomes strong and steady. Then we are able to hold our heads high no matter what happens and know that all is well, because we know how dearly our God loves us. We feel this warm love everywhere within us because God has given us the Holy Spirit. Romans 5:1-5 Life Application Bible.

With this righteousness God has showered us with, we receive the ability to live right with Him and with our mankind. We can now love the things God loves and hate the things He hates. We can go the extra mile where offenses are concerned and forgive others their tresspasses toward us. God's righteousness allows us to see others as He sees them, His creation, loved and made in His own image.

THE RIGHTEOUSNESS OF GOD is where He wants every believer to live. This righteousness that has been bestowed upon us by God, is what we need to live a life free from the power of sin. We can also have freedom from domination of the law, and freedom to become like Christ. Now, we can live in complete submission to Christ, genuinely loving others and using our spiritual gift(s) to serve others and the church of God. We can be good citizens in the world, building up one another in the faith and being sensitive and helpful to those who are weak.

All the subjects we discussed within these pages and so many more that were not discussed tend to block our progress in becoming the people God made us to be. Let us keep our minds and hearts focused on God and His purpose for our lives and let His righteousness accomplish what He intended. Remember, God's standard for righteousness and goodness is extremely high; in fact, it is humanly unattainable.

WE NEED GOD to be the righteous people He wants us to be. That is why he places His righteousness upon us, the believer. It is when we refuse to live as the Word of God instructs us to live that we don't enjoy the blessings God wants to bless us with. Disobedience of God's Word always causes us to forfeit God's blessings.

I trust that you have enjoyed reading this book and its contents have enlightened you. I pray it has you on the path to allow God's righteousness to do a complete work in you. Guard your heart against all the things that can hinder you from receiving God's blessings. Be assured that there are inherent benefits to living in the righteousness God. This righteousness has been shed upon all those that come to Him in faith to be a living sacrifice unto Him.

God's Word tells us that He loves the righteous/upright and they are the eternal object of His care, protection, provision, attention, security, kindness, mercy, and His love. He is righteous and holy, so it is His desire that His people be righteous and holy also.

FOR YOUR READING

Psalms 1:5-6 *Therefore the ungodly shall not stand in the judgment, nor sinners in the congregation of the righteous. For the LORD knoweth the way of the righteous: but the way of the ungodly shall perish.*

Psalm 5:12 *For thou, LORD, wilt bless the righteous; with favour wilt thou compass him as with a shield.*

Psalm 11:7 *For the righteous LORD loveth righteousness; his countenance doth behold the upright.*

Psalms 11:5-6 *The LORD trieth the righteous: but the wicked and him that loveth violence his soul hateth. 6 Upon the wicked he shall rain snares, fire and brimstone, and an horrible tempest: this shall be the portion of their cup.*

Psalm 31:18 *Let the lying lips be put to silence; which speak grievous things proudly and contemptuously against the righteous.*

Psalm 34:15 *The eyes of the LORD are upon the righteous, and his ears are open unto their cry.*

Psalm 34:17 *The righteous cry, and the LORD heareth, and delivereth them out of all their troubles.*

Psalms 34:19-20 *Many are the afflictions of the righteous: but the LORD delivereth him out of them all. He keepeth all his bones: not one of them is broken.*

Psalm 37:29 *The righteous shall inherit the land, and dwell therein for ever.*

Psalm 37:39 *But the salvation of the righteous is of the LORD: he is their strength in the time of trouble.*

Psalm 145:17 *The LORD is righteous in all his ways, and holy in all his works.*

Psalm 146:8 *The LORD openeth the eyes of the blind:*

the LORD raiseth them that are bowed down: the LORD loveth the righteous:

Proverbs 2:7 *He layeth up sound wisdom for the righteous: he is a buckler to them that walk uprightly.*

James 5:16 *Confess your faults one to another, and pray one for another, that ye may be healed. The effectual fervent prayer of a righteous man availeth much.*

I Peter 3:12 *For the eyes of the Lord are over the righteous, and his ears are open unto their prayers: but the face of the Lord is against them that do evil.*

PRAYER: Lord thank you for being a God who loves His people. Thank you for your power and grace, and for your mercy and favor. Thank you that you shower your children with righteousness, and that you want to empower them to live holy lives. Where there is unrighteousness in us, shine your light on it so that we can see it and work to change it. Let us be quick to ask for forgiveness and turn from anything that would be an enemy to the blessings you want to bestow upon us for righteous living. Call out everything that will block us from receiving your blessings. Let us also be quick to tell others of your goodness to us. Let us sing your praises daily as we live and worship, our God. Amen.

MAY OUR PRAYER ALWAYS BE:

May the words of my mouth and the meditation of my heart be pleasing in Your sight, O Lord, my Rock and my Redeemer. Whom have I in heaven but You? And earth has nothing I desire besides You. My flesh and my heart may fail, but God is the strength of my heart and my portion forever.

Show me Your ways, O Lord, teach me Your paths; guide me in Your truth and teach me, for You are my God and my Savior, and my hope is in You all day long. You turned my wailing into dancing; You removed my sackcloth and clothed me with joy, that my heart may sing to You and not be silent. O Lord my God, I will give You thanks forever.

Sing joyfully to the Lord, you righteous; it is fitting for the upright to praise Him. Praise the Lord with the harp; make music to Him on the ten-stringed lyre. Sing to Him a new song; play skillfully, and shout for joy! Why are you so downcast, O my soul? Why so disturbed within me? Put your hope in God, for I will yet praise Him, my Savior and my God.

Because Your love is better than life, my lips will glorify You. I will praise You as long as I live, and in Your name I will lift up my hands. Come let us bow down in worship, let us kneel before the Lord our Maker; for He is our God and we are the people of His pasture, the flock under His care. Praise the Lord, O my soul; all my inmost being, praise His holy name. Praise the Lord, O my soul, and forget not all His benefits - who forgives all your sins and heals all your diseases, who redeems your life from the pit and crowns you with love and compassion, who satisfies your desires with good things so that your youth is renewed like the eagle's. I will extol the Lord at all times; His praise will always be on my lips. My soul will boast in the Lord; let the afflicted hear and rejoice. Glorify the Lord with me; let us exalt His name together.

Search me, O God, and know my heart; test me and know my anxious thoughts. See if there is any offensive way in me, and lead me in the way everlasting. IN THE PRAISE-WORTHY NAME OF JESUS, AMEN.

TO THE READER

I trust that you have been blessed by the truths shared herein. My greatest desire is that you recognize that God's plan for us is that we do not fall prey to the pitfalls which the enemy places in our lives.

At no greater time than **NOW**, is it more imperative that God's people be empowered to live righteously and above every hinderance.

Grace, peace and blessings to each of you.

Made in the USA
San Bernardino, CA
29 April 2017